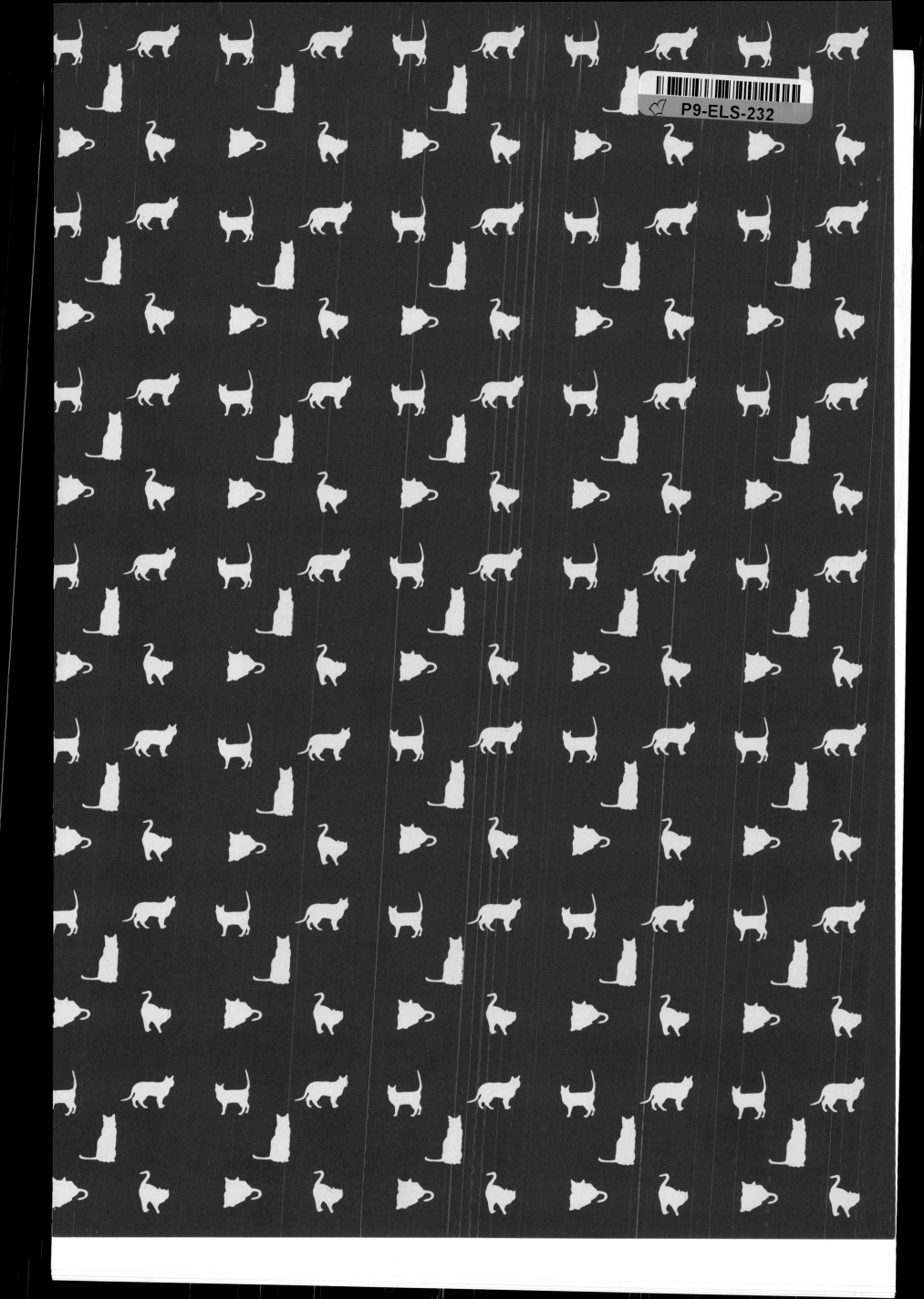

## MAKING FRIENDS

*A*LTHOUGH OFTEN thought of as solitary animals, cats are happier when they have companions – humans, cats, dogs or other pets. A cat should never be left alone for very long periods or it will become unhappy and withdrawn.

*Opposite* A Collie tries to groom a kitten, but the kitten wants only to play.
*Top* Two strange cats meeting, perhaps on the boundary where their territories meet or overlap. Here both are using distinctive body language, to convey a warning, which may prevent a fight.
*Above* I'm not too sure of your intentions!

**Right** The typical pose of a cat
that has just located prey. It
freezes, then looks and listens
intently before creeping
forward.

## FACIAL LANGUAGE

*T*HE CAT has a wide range of facial expressions. Moods can easily be assessed by a quick look at the eyes. The attitude of the ears provides another way to recognize a cat's mood. A contented cat holds its ears upright. When it is cross or about to strike out, the ears are pressed back.

*Opposite* This magnificent ginger tom is slightly apprehensive, as indicated by its tense posture and enquiring whiskers.
*Below* A Longhaired silver tabby feeling rather uncertain. Its eyes are wide and ears are starting to point backwards.

# Kittens

A KITTEN IS a young cat from birth to the age of eight or nine months, at which point it is considered adult.

At birth kittens weigh 3–4 ounces (85–115g); thereafter, due to the richness of their mother's milk, they gain weight very rapidly. Born with tightly sealed eyelids and poor hearing, new kittens are guided and motivated by their strongly developed sense of smell, and move by crawling on their stomachs towards the warmth and comfort of the mother's body; for the first ten days of life they merely suckle and sleep. Gradually the sense of hearing develops and the limbs get stronger. Even before their eyes open, kittens will hiss and spit if lifted from the nest, and during their suckling periods may be heard to purr in a contented way. The mother keeps her kittens spotlessly clean by licking them thoroughly with her rough tongue.

*Opposite* Healthy kittens are playful and adventurous, and benefit from being allowed in the garden from quite young.
*Below* A kitten that strays too far from its mother and litter-mates will become frightened; crying, it will run as fast as it can back to the security of its family.

Once its eyes open, about ten days after birth, the kitten begins to show the first signs of play behaviour, lifting its tiny paws to pat at its mother while she cleans it. As the eyes learn to focus the kitten also starts to pat at its brothers and sisters. By the time it is three weeks old it is able to raise itself up on its legs and toddle around the nest-box.

**Opposite above** Three-week-old kittens spend most of their time sleeping.
**Opposite below** Ten-week sisters finding their way around.
**Above** After periods of play and mischief-making, kittens generally take a nap.
**Left** Even very young kittens show hunting instincts. This youngster exhibits the classic pounce technique.

## NEW SKILLS

*D*URING THE period when they are six to twelve weeks of age, kittens learn a remarkable range of skills. They learn how to run, and they sprint over short distances, stopping, swerving, turning and wheeling. The litter generally splits up into pairs for chasing and boxing games. They leap into the air to avoid capture, and often crouch in corners, making themselves seem as tiny as possible, in order to hide from a pursuer. If there is no escape, kittens try to look as formidable as they can, standing sideways on their tiptoes with the back arched and every hair erect; even the tail is fluffed out, so that it looks like a bottle-brush.

*Above* At eight weeks kittens are very playful and mischievous.
*Opposite* Although kittens love to climb and explore, they often find it difficult to retrace their steps. They cling on with their sharp little claws and cry to be rescued.

## SHORTHAIRED CATS

*W*ITH THE exception of the Russian Blue and the Korat – two breeds of short-coated, light-boned cats with ancient origins, one from Russia and the other from Thailand – the Foreign or Oriental varieties seen in large numbers at today's cat shows are all comparatively modern. Oriental cats were carefully developed from Siamese ancestry by breeders using their knowledge of the genes controlling feline coloration. They managed to produce all manner of combinations of coat colours and patterns while retaining the light bone-structure and typical conformation of the Siamese originals.

*Below* A trio of elegant Oriental tabby kittens looking for all the world like the sacred cats of the Ancient Egyptians.
*Opposite* With the typical stocky build of the British Shorthair breed, here are a Classic (Marbled) silver tabby (on left) and a Spotted silver tabby.
*Inset* Another pedigree of the Shorthair group, a magnificent British Blue.

Cats have two distinct types of sleep, the light variety – taken as a series of catnaps during the day – and deep sleep. During light sleep the cat's blood-pressure remains the same as durings its waking state, the body temperature drops slightly, and the muscles remain mildly tensed. During deep sleep the blood-pressure falls and the temperature rises, while the muscles completely relax. Cats need peace and total security in order to enter this very important deep-sleep phase.

**Right** Cats love basking in the sunshine.
**Far right** A totally relaxed cat settling down to sleep in the warm sunshine.
**Near right** Although its bed of egg trays looks uncomfortable, the cat finds nothing to complain about.

## LIFE IN THE WILD

*W*HEN THEIR owners change homes some cats, for one reason or another, become strays, adding to the already immense stray-cat population. It is rare for a stray cat to try to adopt a new owner, although many caring people take strays into their homes for rehabilitation.

Some cats are feral – that is, they are born to stray parents and remain strays all their lives. Colonies of such cats have their own territories and a well-defined set of feline rules designed for survival.

**Opposite**  It is not a good idea to lock the cat out at night. Night is a dangerous time, and cats should be safely indoors.
**Above**  A kitten unused to confinement tries to climb out of its new garden despite the high mesh fence.

## CAT COLONIES

*H*ORDES OF hungry feral or semi-wild cats forage for their living and forgo the comforts of a caring home. They often live in family groups, usually consisting of sisters and their offspring, with males often leading solitary lives on the outskirts of the group. Feral colonies forage on waste ground and hunt when they can, keeping away from humans.

A complex hierarchy can develop within such a feline colony. Once the pecking-order has been established, all the cats within the group seem to accept their rankings and live contentedly. On the peripheries, the tom cats likewise sort out individual ranking and status, generally by fighting to establish position. They mark the boundaries of their territories and guard them jealously against interlopers.

*Right* Feral cats, drawn by the strong smell of fish, gather round hoping for a free hand-out.
*Below* In stark contrast to the cats from a colony, these well-fed tabbies relax in front of a blazing fire after a substantial meal.
*Following page* The identical markings and brilliant green eyes of these two beautiful ginger-and-white cats indicate that they are almost certainly litter-brothers.

## THE HUNTING TERRITORY

*A*LMOST EVERY cat will be an active hunter if given the opportunity; neutered pet cats hunt just as seriously as their entire or feral counterparts, although an over-pampered and overweight cat may well be too sluggish to enjoy the thrill of the chase. A radius of about fifty yards around the cat's home will define its natural boundary, and most cats confine their hunting to this area. Farm cats often extend their hunting to fields and woodlands adjoining their territories, and this may lead to fights with neighbouring cats.

Most hunting takes place at night, unless the cat is kept in. Cats have good night vision, and acute hearing in a range beyond that of a human ear. In urban areas cats hunt rodents and birds, while the country cat has a broader range: hares, frogs, fish, snakes and large insects in addition to rats, mice, bats and a wide variety of birds. Pet cats often bring their prey home and proudly present it to their owners.

*Right* A tortoiseshell Shorthair on a hunting expedition.
*Below* For a cat in full chase after its prey, a stream presents no obstacle.

**Above** On many farms the cats are often mostly of the same type, being closely related to each other in a hopelessly tangled family tree. Ginger cats are generally males.

**Right** This tortoiseshell colouring is found only in females. It is caused by an unusual sex-linked gene, which produces ginger males and tortoiseshell females in the same litter.

**Opposite** Wherever there are horses there are bound to be lots of mice and rats, drawn by the corn in the feed store. Cats act as the perfect pest control, and often make equine friends.

**Right** Surveying the landscape from the top of a haystack.

## YESTERDAY, TODAY, TOMORROW

*I*N THIS book you have seen how the cat has managed to remain virtually unchanged through the ages, still being as self-possessed and independent as ever. Although cats tolerate the relationship with humans and are prepared to enjoy the comforts of a good home, the inborn behaviour patterns of their wild ancestors lurk just below the domesticated veneer. The cat of today retains the hunting skills and physical prowess of its forebears: even the most pampered puss will, given the opportunity, react to the thrill of the hunt.

No other pet is as fastidious in its habits, and having a cat in the home is both rewarding and therapeutic.

*Opposite* The cat's natural coat provides perfect insulation against extremes of heat and cold.
*Above* Cats are keen to hunt, even in snow, but are less fond of rain, which quickly soaks their outer coat.
*Following page* There is nothing quite so disdainful as a cat walking slowly away, refusing all friendly advances.